GUITAR Practice & TECHNIQUE METHOD 1

TERRY CARTER

ROCKLIKETHEPROS

ROCK LIKE THE PROS

CONTENTS

ISBN-13: **978-1-7359692-6-8**
Copyright 2021

TERRY CARTER
ROCKLIKETHEPROS**.COM**

DESIGNED BY **M.** @itsMariWay

WHAT WE HAVE FOR YOU!

THE ESSENTIALS	A
HOW TO READ TAB	B
GUITAR PARTS	C
GUITAR HANDS	D
NOTES ON THE GUITAR NECK	E
UNDERSANDING CHORD DIAGRAMS	F
MUSIC SYMBOLS TO KNOW	G
GUITAR CHORD CHART	I
HOW TO HOLD A PICK	01
PRACTICE & TECHNIQUE BOOTCAMP	02
01 - **LESSON 01**	05
02 - **LESSON 02**	07
03 - **LESSON 03**	09
04 - **LESSON 04**	11
05 - **LESSON 05**	13
06 - **LESSON 06**	15
07 - **LESSON 07**	17
08 - **LESSON 08**	19
09 - **LESSON 09**	21
10 - **LESSON 10**	27
11 - **WRITE YOUR OWN EXERCISE**	23
TERRY CARTER's MESSAGE FOR YOU	27
ABOUT THE AUTHOR	K
ALL YOUR GUITAR NEEDS	L
ABOUT UKE LIKE THE PROS	M

THE ESSENTIALS

It is important to learn and memorize these terms and symbols because they not only apply to guitar but to all music.

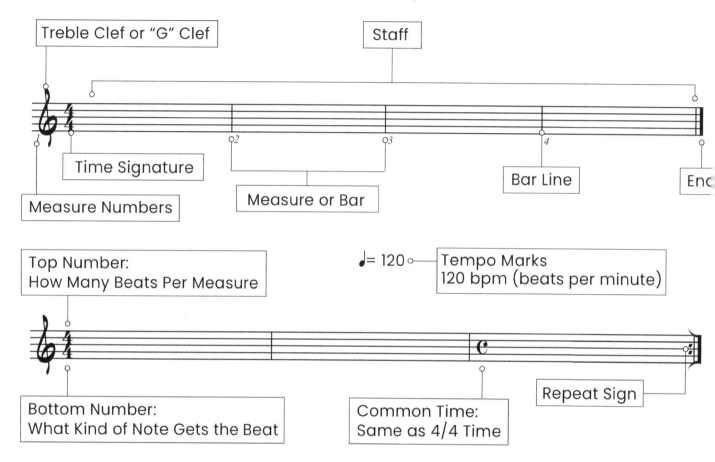

Notes On The Staff: There are seven notes in music (A, B, C, D, E, F, G) and they move up and down alphabetically on the staff.

How To Remember The Notes:

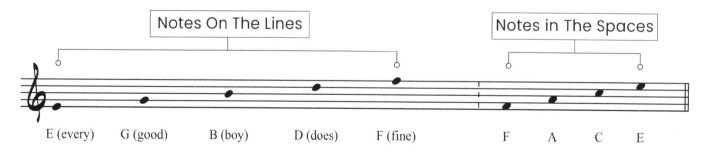

HOW TO READ TAB

Tablature (TAB) is a form of music reading for guitar that uses a 6 line staff and numbers. Each line of the staff represents a string on the guitar and the numbers represent which fret you play on. When looking at the TAB staff it reads like it's upside down on the paper compared to the strings of your guitar. On the TAB staff, the highest line represents the 1st string (E string) of the guitar, while the lowest line represents the 6th string (E string) of the guitar. When you see 2 or more notes stacked on top of each other on the TAB staff, that means you play those notes at the same time, like a a chord.

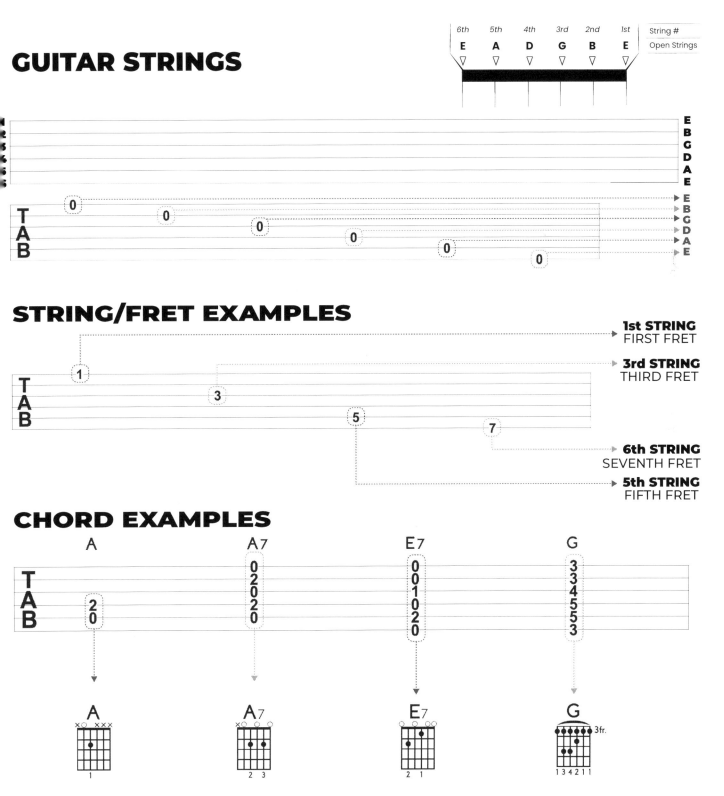

GUITAR PARTS

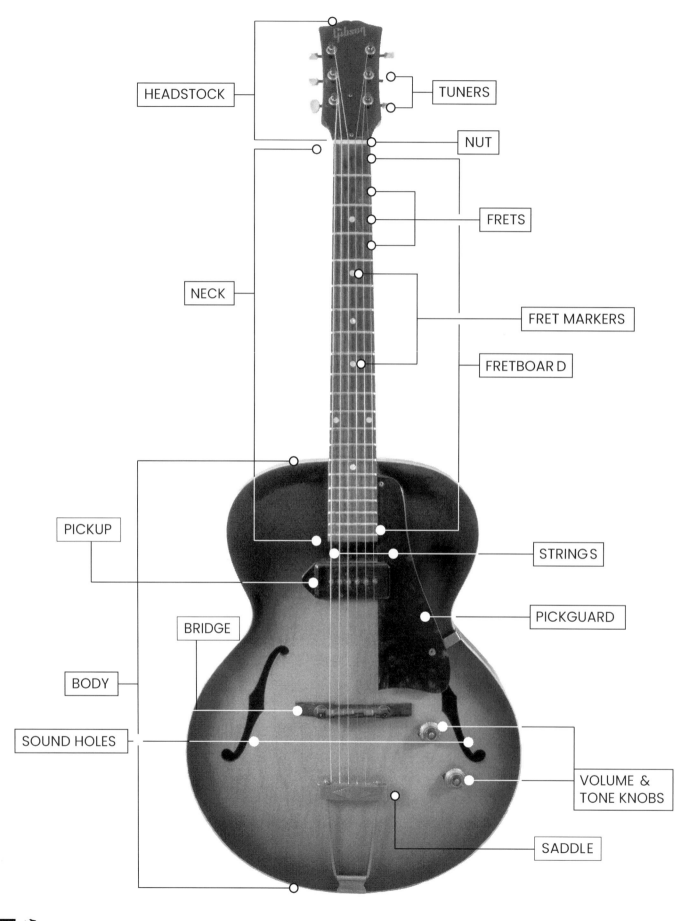

GUITAR HANDS

When playing fingerstyle on your guitar, you will see both letters and numbers to indicate which fingers to use both for picking hand and your fretting hand. These letters and numbers will show up in the music notation, TAB, and/or chord diagrams.

FRETTING HAND	PICKING HAND
The left hand for right-handed players, will be indicated in the music or chord diagrams by numbers: **1**=Index finger **3**=Ring finger **2**=Middle finger **4**=Pinky finger	The right hand for right-handed players, will be indicated in the music by letters: **p**=Thumb **m**=middle **i**=index **a**=ring **c**=pinky (not used in this course)

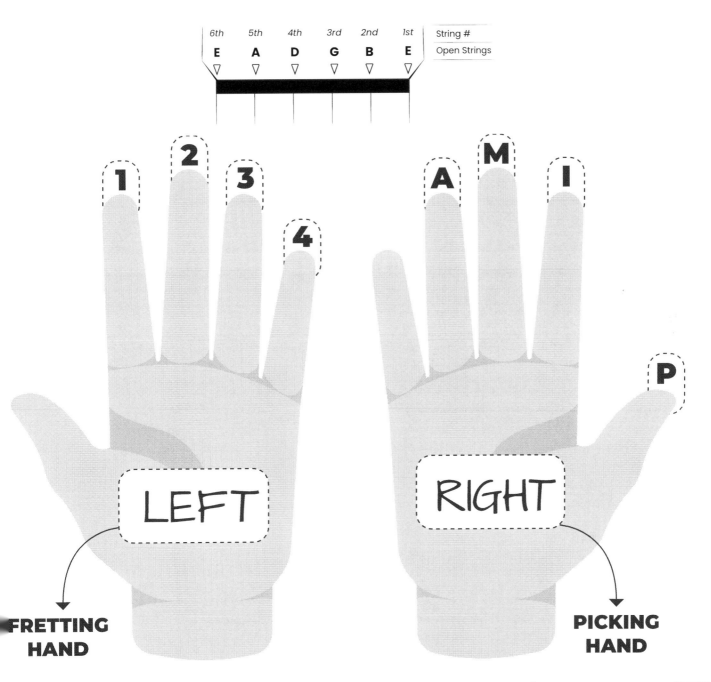

FRETTING HAND — LEFT

PICKING HAND — RIGHT

ROCKLIKETHEPROS D

NOTES ON THE GUITAR NECK

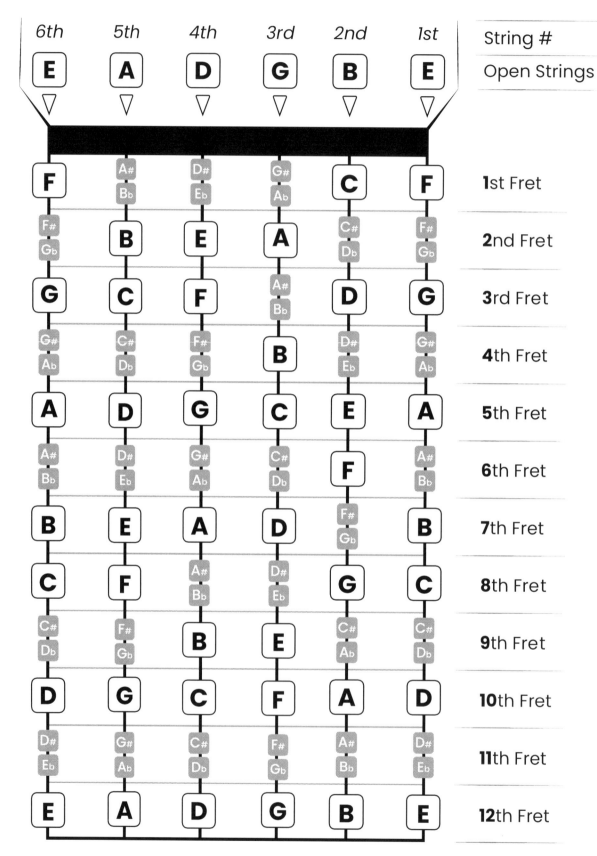

Notes repeat at 12th Fret

UNDERSTANDING CHORD DIAGRAMS

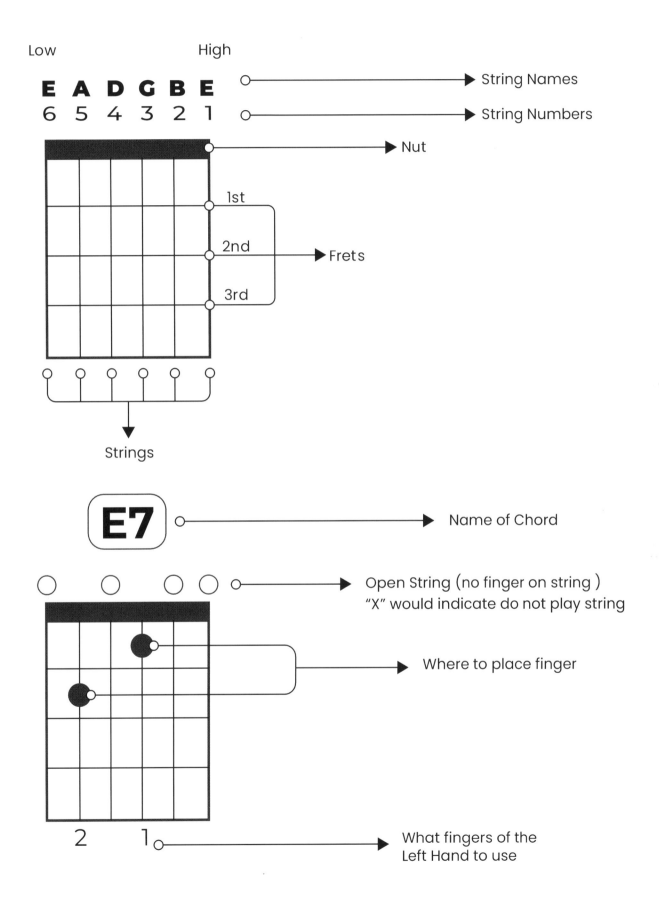

MUSIC SYMBOLS TO KNOW

A variety of symbols, articulations, repeats, hammer on's, pull off's, bends, and slides.

 **Fermata:** Hold note

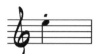 **Staccato:** Play note short

 **Accent:** Play note loud

 **Accented Staccato:** Play note loud + short

 Vibrato Rapid "shaking" of note

 **Arpeggiated Chord:** Play the notes in fast succession from low to high strings

 **Grace Note:** Fast embellishment note played before the main note

 **Mute:** "Muffle" sound of strings either with left or right hand

 **Down Stroke:** Pick string(s) with a downward motion

 **Up Stroke:** Pick string(s) with an upward motion

Tie: Play first note but do not play second note that it is tied to

Ledger Lines: Extend the staff higher or lower.

Slash Notation: Repeat notes & rhythms from previous measure

1 Bar Repeat: Repeat notes & rhythms from previous measure

2 Bar Repeat: Repeat notes & rhythms from previous 2 measures

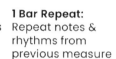

Repeat Sign: (Beginning)

Repeat Sign: (End)

1st Ending: Play this part the first time only

2nd Ending: Play this part the second time

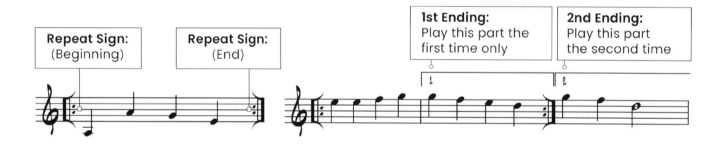

(D.C. AL FINE) — *D.C.* (da capo) means go to the beginning of the tune and stop when you get to *Fine*

(D.C. AL CODA) — *D.C.* means go to the beginning of the tune and jump to *Coda* ⊕ when you see the sign ⊕

(D.S. AL FINE) — *D.S.* (dal segno) means go to the *Sign* 𝄋 and stop when you get to *Fine*

(D.S. AL CODA) — *D.S.* means go to the *Sign* 𝄋 And Jump to the *Coda* ⊕ when you see ⊕

SIM... — Play the same rhythm, strum pattern, or picking pattern as the previous measure

ETC... — Continue the same rhythm, strum pattern, or picking pattern as the previous measure

Hammer On:
Pick first note then hammer on to the next note without picking it.

Pull Off:
Pick first note then pull off to the next note without picking it.

Hammer On & Pull Off:
Pick first note, hammer on to the next note, and pull off to the last note all in one motion.

1/2 Step Bend:
Bend the first note a 1/2 step or 1 fret.

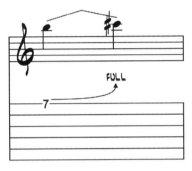

Whole Step Bend:
Bend the first note a whole step or 2 frets.

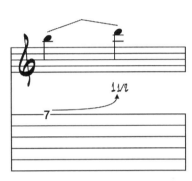

Step & 1/2 Bend:
Bend the first note 1 1/2 steps or 3 frets

Forward Slide:
Pick first note and slide up to higher note.

Backward Slide:
Pick first note and slide back to lower note.

Forward/Backward Slide:
Pick first note, slide up to next note and then slide back.

Slide Into Note:
Slide from 2-3 frets below note

Slide Off Note:
Slide off 2-5 frets after note

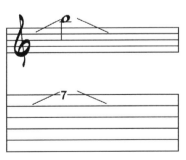

Slide Into Note then Slide Off Note

GUITAR CHORD CHART

These are some of the most widely used chords in all of music. Although there are more chords than what is listed, these chords represent the most widely used shapes.
The string names (from high to low) are:

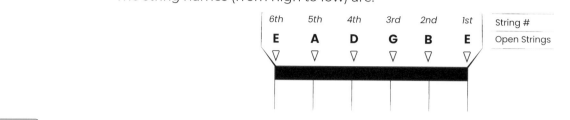

MAJOR CHORDS

MINOR CHORDS

DOMINANT 7th CHORDS

ROCKLIKETHEPROS

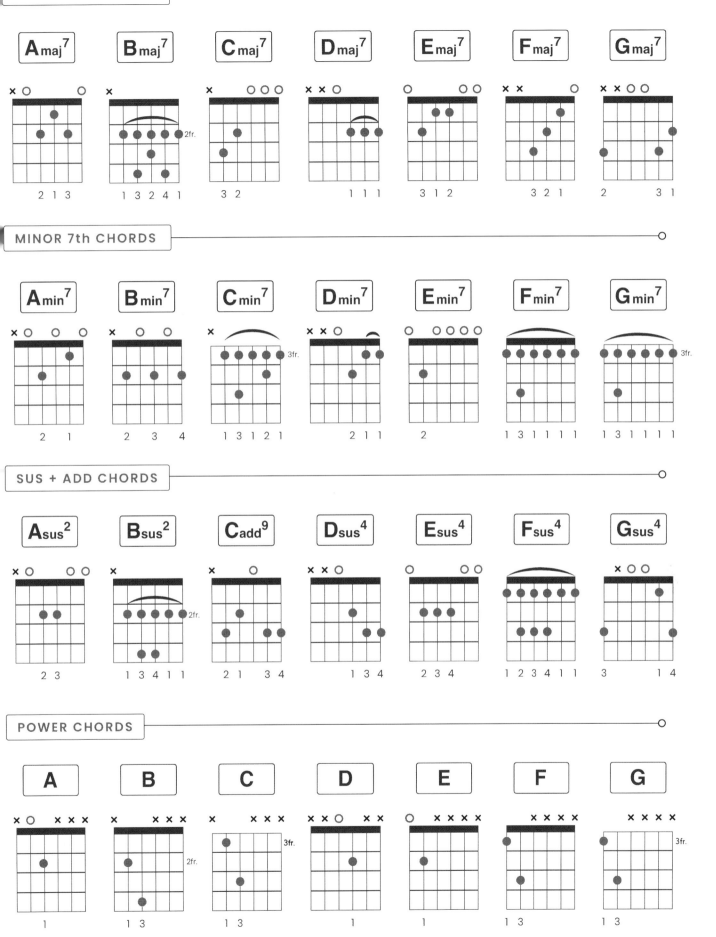

HOW TO HOLD A PICK

Playing with a pick is one of the main ways to play the guitar. There are many different types of picks out there, made of different materials, thicknesses, and shapes. There is no right or wrong pick, it's simply the pick that feels comfortable and sounds pleasing to your style. A good place to start is a Rock Like The Pros pick, available at **store.rocklikethepros.com**.

To hold the pick, grip it between your thumb and index finger. You need to grip it tight enough so that it doesn't slide around when you play, but not so tight that you are feeling strain in your fingers or wrists. A good place to strum the guitar is halfway between the end of the fretboard and the bridge. Most likely this will be towards the bottom of the soundhole.

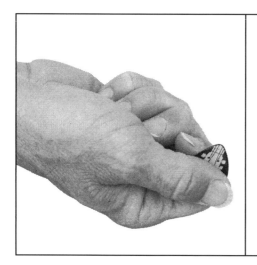  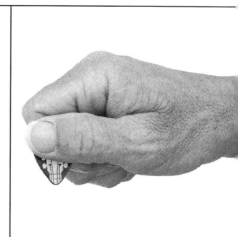

Remember: In the **#1 Guitar & Ukulele Store** you can find everything you've been looking for:

- Guitars, Ukuleles, Baritone Ukuleles and Guitarleles.
- Gig Bags and Hard Shell Cases.
- Stands and Straps.
- Capos, Tunners and Strings.
- Electronic Devices.
- Books... and more!

store.**ROCKLIKETHEPROS.COM**

GUITAR Practice & TECHNIQUE METHOD 1

Do you struggle with your technique on your guitar? Do you wish you could play with more speed, accuracy, dexterity, and confidence? The Rock Like The Pros Beginning **Guitar Practice and Technique Method 1** book will not only help you develop killer technique and strength, but will give you some amazing warm-up exercises you can do every time you pick up your guitar.

This book will guide you step-by-step through the very best guitar exercises that will build up your technique in both your right and left hands. Each lesson will progressively get more difficult, building upon the techniques you learned in the previous lesson. This Beginning Guitar Practice and Technique Method 1 has helped thousands of students, many of them just like you, gain better control and skills on their guitar.

Are you a beginner? Perfect. This technique method was written for you, and will start from the beginning and gradually help you increase your skills and ability. Don't worry if you have been playing guitar a while because with the play-along backing tracks you can practice each exercise at the appropriate tempo that fits your skill level. These are the same exercises that are used by the pros when they warm up and want to increase their technique.

With this book you get free access to the all the backing tracks for each lesson. You will be able to download the slow, medium, and fast backing tracks, as well as the extended long backing tracks, so you can work these exercises up and down the fretboard at your own speed. For instant access to the backing tracks, visit **rocklikethepros.com/method-1**.

There is also an accompanying video instructional course (sold separately) that compliments this book, available at **rocklikethepros.com/courses**

The techniques you learn in this book can be used daily as you continue to develop more speed and accuracy in you playing. You will also notice these techniques will help all aspects of your guitar playing, such as your strumming, fingerpicking, soloing, and chord melodies.

Plus, while you are learning and practicing these exercises, you will see massive improvement in your eye-hand coordination and your ear training. Since many of these patterns are repetitive as they move to different strings and frets, your ear will guide you and let you know if you are playing the exercises correctly.

Need help learning the guitar fretboard? All the techniques you will learn in the Beginning Guitar Practice and Technique Method 1 will work up and down the neck, you will gain an improved knowledge and ability to play both horizontally and vertically up the guitar neck.

You will develop speed and technique in both your left and right hands. You will see massive improvement in your 1st, 2nd, 3rd, and 4th fingers, and your picking hand, while you work on chromatic notes, leaps, jumps, slides, and spider exercises.

This will be the greatest book you can find for your guitar playing that will build your technique so you can become the guitar player that you know you can be. Sound too good to be true? It's not.

The Beginning Guitar Practice and Technique Method 1 is the most amazing book to build your strength and technique on the guitar. Each lesson was been hand-crafted for you by guitar master, Terry Carter. Terry is the founder of rocklikethepros.com, and has taken the techniques that helped him become the #1 online guitar instructor and put them into one comprehensive book.

Terry spent over 20 years as a Los Angeles studio musician, producer, and writer, working with greats such as Weezer, Josh Groban, Robby Krieger (The Doors), 2-time Grammy winning composer Christopher Tin (Calling All Dawns), Duff McKagan (Guns N' Roses), Grammy winning producer Charles Goodan (Santana/Rolling Stones), and the Los Angeles Philharmonic.

erry has written and produced tracks for commercials (Discount Tire and Puma) and TV shows, including Scorpion (CBS), Pit Bulls & Parolees (Animal Planet), Trippin', Wildboyz, and The Real World (MTV). He has published over 12 books for Rock Like The Pros and Uke Like The Pros, filmed over 30 guitar and ukulele online courses, and has over 15 million views on his Rock Like The Pros and Uke Like The Pros and Rock Like The Pros social media channels. Jerry received a Master of Music in Studio/Jazz Guitar Performance from University of Southern California, and a Bachelor of Music from San Diego State University, with an emphasis in Jazz Studies and Music Education. He has taught at the University of Southern California, San Diego State University, Santa Monica College, Miracosta College, and Los Angeles Trade Tech College.

Let's dive into the Beginning Guitar Practice and Technique Method 1.

Sounds Good?

Well, it's time. There is nothing more I can say that will help you become a great Guitar player. It's now your turn to dive into the *Guitar Practice & Technique Method 1!*

PREMIUM MEMBERSHIP

ACCESS TO ALL OUR COURSES - LIVE ZOOM CALLS - STORE DISCOUNTS
ROCK LIKE THE PROS NATION - FORUM - GIVEAWAYS - CHALLENGES
... AND MORE!

LESSON 01 *PAGE 01 OF 02*

This exercise will help you develop your strength and independence of your 1st and 2nd fingers. Start on the 1st fret of the 1st string with your 1st finger and then move up to the 2nd fret with your 2nd finger. Do the same pattern on the 2nd, 3rd, 4th, 5th and 6th strings, then move the pattern up one fret so you will play on the 6th string, 2nd and 3rd frets. Take the pattern down the 5th, 4th, 3rd, 2nd, and 1st strings, and then move up to the 3rd fret and do it all again until you work up to the 5th fret.

LESSON 02 *PAGE 01 OF 02*

This exercise will be the same as the previous except you will use your 1st and 3rd fingers. Start on the 1st fret of the 1st string with your 1st finger and then move up to the 3nd fret with your 3rd finger. Do the same pattern on the 2nd, 3rd, 4th, 5th, and 6th strings, then move the pattern up one fret so you will play on the 6th string, 2nd and 4th frets. Take the pattern down the 5th, 4th, 3rd, 2nd, and 1st strings and then move up to the 3rd fret and do it all again until you work up to the 5th fret.

You can post your progress and see how others are doing at the ROCKLIKETHEPROS.COM Forum.

You can also get free access to the backing tracks at:
ROCKLIKETHEPROS.COM/METHOD-1

LESSON 03 *PAGE 01 OF 02*

We will continue the same vibe as the previous lesson except you will use your 1st and 4th fingers. Typically our pinky or 4th finger is our weakest finger. Start on the 1st fret of the 1st string with your 1st finger and then move up to the 4th fret with your 4th finger. Do the same pattern on the 2nd, 3rd, 4th, 5th, and 6th strings, then move the pattern up one fret so you will play on the 6th string, 2nd and 5th frets. Take the pattern down the 5th, 4th, 3rd, 2nd, and 1st strings and then move up to the 3rd fret and do it all again until you work up to the 5th fret.

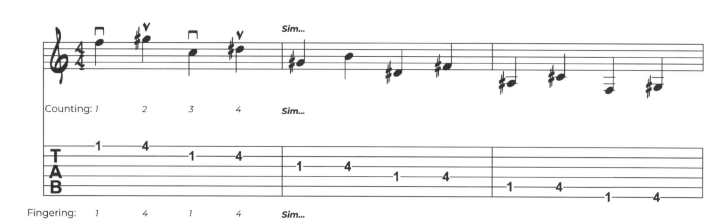

PRACTICE TIP:

Practice all these exercises slowly to make sure you play them correctly, accurately, and with the proper fingers.

LESSON 04 *PAGE 01 OF 02*

This is the granddaddy of all technique exercises. It is the most common one that will help you build strength and speed in all fingers and serve as a great warmup whenever you pick up your guitar. Start on the 1st fret of the 1st string with your 1st finger, then add your second finger to the 2nd fret, 3rd finger to the 3rd fret, and 4th finger to the 4th fret. Then move up to the 2nd string and do it all again up all the strings. Once you finish up the 6th string move up to the 2nd fret and start the pattern back down all the strings.

Remember: In the **#1 Guitar & Ukulele Store** you can find everything you've been looking for:

Guitars, Ukuleles, Baritone Ukuleles and Guitarleles.
Gig Bags and Hard Shell Cases.
Stands and Straps.
Capos, Tunners and Strings.
Electronic Devices.
Books... and more!

store.**ROCKLIKETHEPROS.COM**

LESSON 05 *PAGE 01 OF 02*

The backward granddaddy. This lesson will be in reverse of the previous lesson as we start on the 1st string with our 4th finger on the 4th fret, and move down to the 3rd finger 3rd fret, 2nd finger 2nd fret, and 1st finger on the 1st fret. Then move up to the 2nd string, but remember to start the pattern with your 4th finger on the 4th fret. Continue through all the strings, and when you finish the 6th string, move your pinky up to the 5th fret and continue the same backward pattern down all the strings.

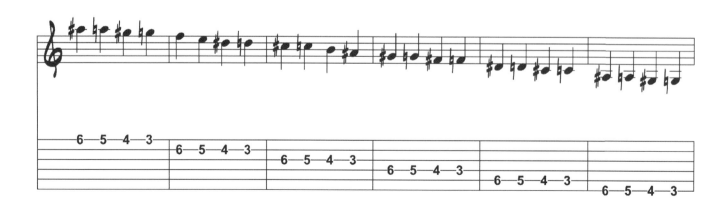

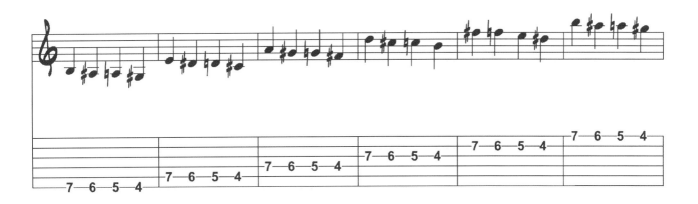

PRACTICE TIP:

The thumb of your fretting hand should be there for support and guidance. If you are feeling any pain from squeezing the neck too hard, make sure to lighten up your grip.

LESSON 06 *PAGE 01 OF 02*

It's time to mix it up and try some different combinations of your 1st, 2nd, 3rd, and 4th fingers. Start on the 1st string with your 1st finger on the 1st fret, followed by 3rd finger on the 3rd fret, 2nd finger on the 2nd fret, and 4th finger on the 4th fret. By simply mixing up the order you play your fingers, you will see increased mobility and strength. Play this pattern up all the strings and then move up to the 2nd fret and repeat it moving down the strings.

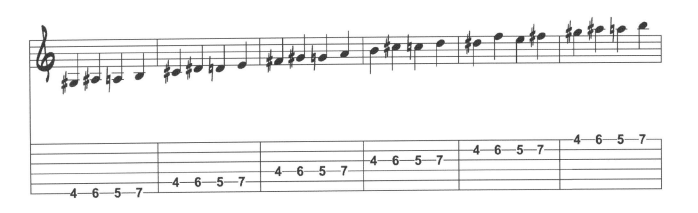

PRACTICE TIP:

To increase your speed and accuracy, play each note on your fingertips with each joint of your fingers curved.

LESSON 07 *PAGE 01 OF 02*

There is one more variation you can do with your 1st, 2nd, 3rd, and 4th fingers. Start on the 1st string with your 1st finger on the 1st fret, jump up to the 4th finger on the 4th fret, 2nd finger on the 2nd fret, and 3rd finger on the 3rd fret. The stretch between your 1st and 4th finger will help build your dexterity and finger strength. Play this pattern up all the strings, and then move up to the 2nd fret and repeat it moving down the strings.

Remember: In the **#1 Guitar & Ukulele Store** you can find everything you've been looking for:

- Guitars, Ukuleles, Baritone Ukuleles and Guitarleles.
- Gig Bags and Hard Shell Cases.
- Stands and Straps.
- Capos, Tunners and Strings.
- Electronic Devices.
- Books... and more!

store.**ROCKLIKE**THEPROS**.COM**

LESSON 08 *PAGE 01 OF 02*

This is one of the greatest technique exercises I have ever written. It was originally written while I was a college guitar professor at Santa Monica College. This one will work all 4 of your fingers moving up and down the fretboard. Start with playing on the 1st string, frets 1-2-3-4, then slide your 4th finger from the 4th fret to the 5th fret and walk the fingers down to frets 5-4-3-2, then slide the 1st finger up to the 3rd fret and continue this pattern up the neck until you get to the 13th fret. Then you will work the pattern in reverse as you work back down to the starting note on the 1st fret.

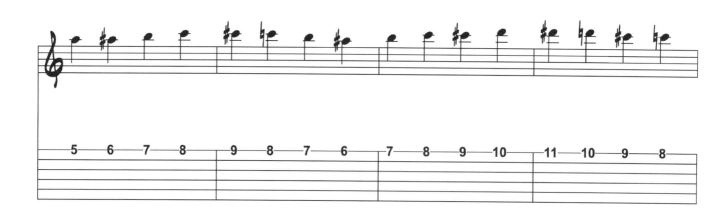

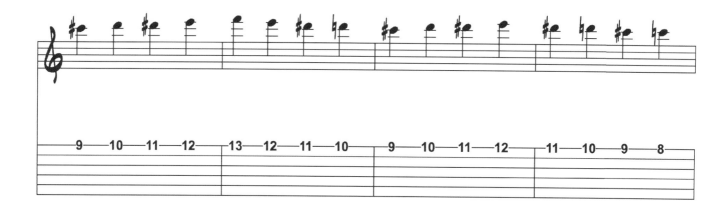

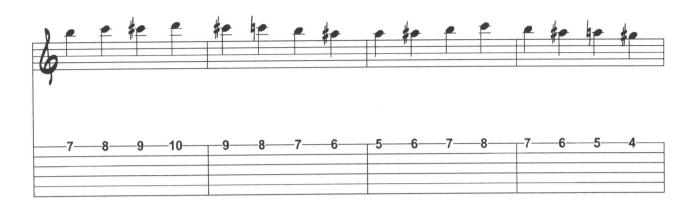

LESSON 09 PAGE 01 OF 06

You are going to take the exercise from the previous lesson and expand it to all 6 strings. This one exercise will help you gain control on all the strings on every fret up and down the neck. This will be one of the most useful technique builders you can do for your playing; make sure to do it daily.

1st String

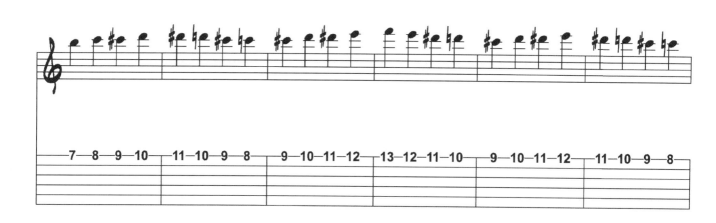

2nd String

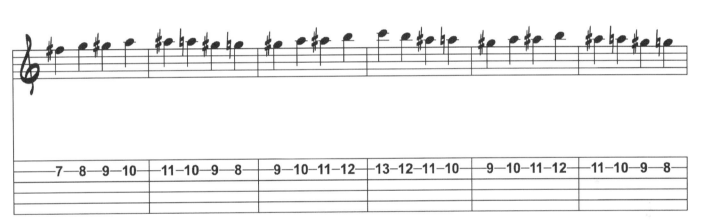
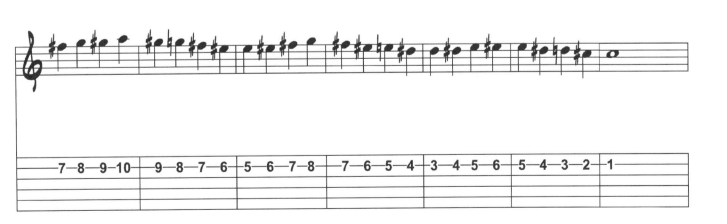

3rd String

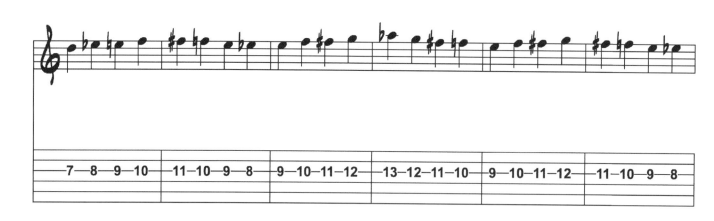

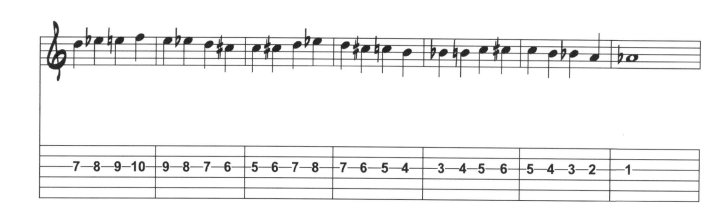

4th String

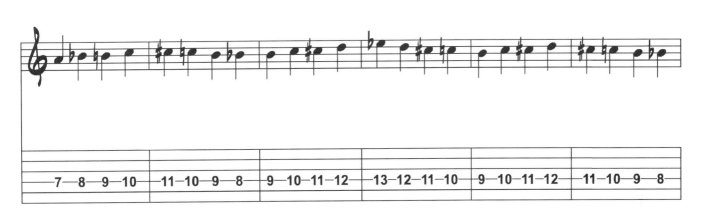

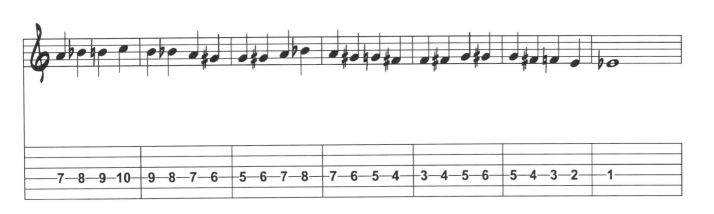

5th String

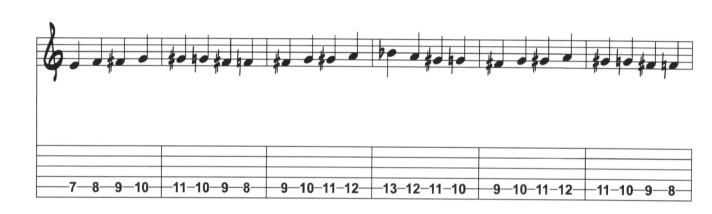

6th String

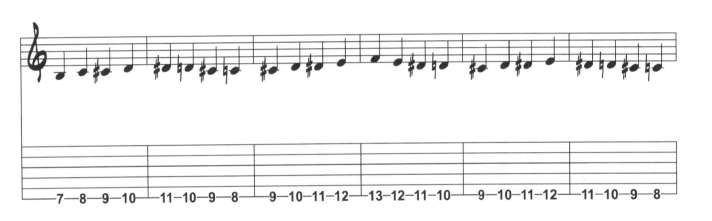

LESSON 10

This is a Spider exercise I call "Spiderwalk." This lesson will use 2 notes at a time moving in contrary (opposite) motion. It will start with a pinch on the 5th string 3rd fret and 2nd string 1st fret, then move to 5th string 2nd fret and 2nd string 3rd fret, followed by 5th string 1st fret and 2nd string 4th fret, and then finish up with 6th string 5th fret and 2nd string 5th fret. Then take this exact pattern and repeat it up one fret.

WHAT THE STUDENTS SAY:

I want to share with you how happy I am to be playing More guitar again! This Practice & Technique Method 1 really jump started me! I dug out some old flat pick guitar magazines that are like new because they were way too advanced for me at the time, but since taking over a year and a half of Ukulele Lessons with Terry Carter I actually am able to play some of the exercises and songs! Thank you!

GUITAR STUDENT.

LESSON 11 *PAGE 01 OF 02*

There are endless finger and fret combinations that can be used as practice and technique builders. It's time for you to get creative and write your very own technique exercise. There is no right or wrong as long as you dig playing what you write. Remember that simpler is sometimes better.

LESSON 11 *PAGE 02 OF 02*

GREAT *job!*

Congratulations for making it to the end of the Rock Like The Pros Beginning Guitar Practice and Technique Method 1. This is not an easy book to get through, but you should have seen improved technique, speed, strength, coordination, dexterity, and confidence. You also have a bunch of amazing warm-up exercises you can do every time you pick up your guitar. Continue to work on these lessons at faster tempos, always improving your tone, tempo, and accuracy.

Did you enjoy this material? Wondering what is next?

Here at Rock Like The Pros we take guitar very seriously, making sure to help you become the guitar player that you know you can be. This is why we offer the Premium Membership at rocklikethepros.com. The Premium Membership not only gives you access to all of our online guitar courses, downloadable TAB, Backing Tracks, but also access to the RLTP Nation. The RLTP Nation is the worldwide community of guitar players who have, many just like you, dedicated themselves to learning and growing as a musician. With your Premium Membership you get access to the LIVE Q & A that we do with all our members, access to the Member Only Forum, Challenges and Giveaways. You will have the chance to connect with the entire RLTP Nation, including the fantastic team here are Rock Like The Pros. Come on over to rocklikethepros.com and get your free trial to the **Rock Like The Pros Premium Membership**

I'm proud of you for completing the Beginning Guitar Practice and Technique Method 1, and I look forward to connecting with you as a Premium Member.

Talk soon,
Terry Carter

ABOUT THE AUTHOR

TERRY CARTER

Terry Carter is a San Diego-based Guitar and Ukulele player, surfer, songwriter, and creator of Rock Like Th Pros and Uke Like The Pros. Terry has worked with Weezer, Josh Groban, Robby Krieger (The Doors), 2 time Grammy winner composer Christopher Tin (Calling All Dawns), and the Los Angeles Philharmonic. Terry has written and produced tracks for commercials (Puma and Discount Tire) and various television shows, including Scorpion (CBS), Pit Bulls & Parolees (Animal Planet), Trippin' and Wildboyz and The Real World (MTV).
Terry received a Masters of Music in Studio/Jazz Guita Performance from University of Southern California and a Bachelor of Music from San Diego State University, with an emphasis in Jazz Studies and Music Education.

ALL YOUR GUITAR NEEDS AT
store.ROCKLIKETHEPROS.COM

Electro Acoustic Guitars

Acoustic Guitars

Guitarleles / Guileles

Amplifiers and Pedals

Guitar Books

Guitar, Ukulele, Guitarlele and Baritone ACCESSORIES

ABOUT ROCKLIKETHEPROS.COM

The perfect place to learn how to play Guitar!

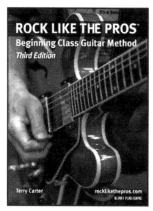

Beginning
Class Guitar Method

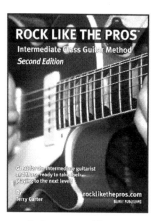

Intermediate
Class Guitar Method

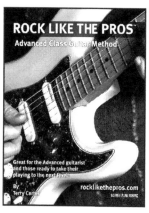

Advanced
Class Guitar Method

Beginning Blues Guitar Mastery

Strumming Mastery for Guitar

20 Most Important Strum Patterns

Premium Membership

ROCKLIKETHEPROS.COM
store.ROCKLIKETHEPROS.COM

@rocklikethepros

INTERESTED IN **UKULELE CONTENT?**

UKELIKETHEPROS.COM

Made in the USA
Columbia, SC
12 January 2022